# REBEL ENTREPRENEUR

## BY

## ARNON BARNES

Ordering Information:
Quantity sales. Special discounts are available on quantity purchases by corporations, associations, and others. Orders by U.S. trade bookstores and wholesalers. Please contact Arnon Barnes via
www.BusinessRebelMasterClass.com/

Edited and Marketed By
DreamStarters University
www.DreamStartersUniversity.com

# ACKNOWLEDGMENTS

First, I want to start this book with gratitude. Gratitude towards you, the reader. Gratitude to the entrepreneur inside of you - the entrepreneur who never gives up, the entrepreneur who never throws in the towel, the one always looking to solve problems and make this world a better place. Thank you for picking up this book. Out of the thousands of books out there on business and entrepreneurship, you found mine. Thank you for giving me the opportunity to make a positive impact on your life, your business, and your bank account.

My goal with this book is simple: I want you to have at least one insight, one "aha" moment, or make one distinction that will change the way you play the business game forever. When you experience that one 'game-changer' insight from reading this book, then I will consider my mission accomplished. Of course, I hope that you end up with more than one, however, sometimes all you need is one new action that will help take your business to the next level.

Secondly, I want to acknowledge all my teachers over the years that have shared their knowledge and expertise with me. To be clear, I am not going to proclaim that everything in this book is my own material. Some if it is, but some of it is from years of studying, learning and implementing ideas from other pioneers in the arena of business and personal development. To all my teachers and coaches - Tony Robbins, T. Harv Eker, Jack Canfield, Keith Cunningham, Grant Cardone, Robert Kiyosaki and Jim Rohn, thank you for the lessons and guidance.

Finally, I want to thank my team for supporting and believing in me. Thank you for having my back in the good, bad, and ugly times. Your support has played a major part in the creation of this book and my work.

A special word of thanks to Judith for always having my corner and being my rock. I love you always.

And to my son Joshua, abba is proud of you. Thank you for being the light in my life and being the gift that you are. You are my hero.

# Table of Contents

# Chapter 1

# The Way of the Rebel Entrepreneur

There are many kinds of entrepreneurs in this world. They all have different personalities, mindsets and approaches. One thing I've come to learn and understand from coaching and training tens of thousands of people from all over the world is that everyone is unique.

I've had the privilege to have coached people from everywhere, all walks of life. People from places like Brazil, South Africa, Poland, Italy, the Netherlands, Israel, Belgium, United Kingdom, Germany and Singapore to name a few. By far, the most obvious thing I've noticed in working with so many people with so many different backgrounds is this: there is no cookie-cutter system for achieving success.

Having said that, it is true that there are certain commonalities successful and wealthy people share. I've discovered these by watching the rich and analyzing what they do and how they do it, how they really play the game.

Let's take a step back and start with this basic understanding. Business and life are just games. And the game of business is all about seeing things differently than most people. I first realized this when I was a young kid.

Back then, I remember seeing my dad buying and working on old, beat-up properties. And my mom never understood it. She never really wanted to get too involved with what my dad was doing, because all she could see was the beginning. What she saw in her mind was my dad spending money on some shitty, run down properties that weren't really worth much.

But my dad saw things differently. He saw the finished product in his head. He saw the possibilities. He saw the opportunity. He knew if he invested his time and energy, he could turn a profit. He knew what other people saw as a waste of time was really a gold mine waiting to be cracked open.

At age 11, I discovered my own gold mine. My uncle owned a toy store, and he would often sell me toys from his store at a discount. It wasn't long before I figured out I could sell the toys I'd gotten at a discount for a little bit higher price to my classmates, and make some money.

As a kid, this is how I got started playing the game of business. Now, many years later, I've come to understand there are many different ways to play the business game. The first way you can play the game of business is you can refuse. In fact, over 80% of the world's population refuses to play the business game.

There are good people with good hearts and good intentions out there who simply refuse to play the game. If we're talking about the game of business specifically, there are people out there who simply say, "Look, business is not for me. I want to be an employee. I want the security. I want the consistent paychecks. At the end of the month, I want to know I'm for sure going to get 'X' amount of money."

So, basically, this type of person makes a conscious refusal of getting involved in the business game. This type of person says, "Listen, business is not for me. I know who I am, and who I am doesn't want any part of that." There's one major flaw with this philosophy---over 90% of all millionaires made their money by owning a business.

There is another type of person who makes an unconscious refusal of playing the business game. This person's refusal looks more like this: I wake up; I go to school; finish school; I get a job; I retire at some point. This is

"buy-in" to the way of the system. This is doing what

you're told to do and not questioning if there might be a better, faster and more abundant way to make money and live the lifestyle you desire and deserve.

Both of these types of people are flat out refusing to play the business game. My purpose here is not to say whether what these people are doing is good or bad, right or wrong. I'm simply saying refusal is one-way people play the game.

The second way to play the business game---and this is how a lot of people play it---is the way of the pretender. The pretender pretends to be in business. They pretend to be an entrepreneur. They pretend to be making millions.

It is very easy to identify a pretender. Pretenders are normally very, very busy people. In fact, they are so busy being busy that they are too busy to make any money at all. That's how busy they are. They haven't got the time for money. That's the first way you can easily identify a pretender.

Maybe you've met some people like this in your life. This type of person is someone you know and run into occasionally, and when you do, you ask, "Hey, how is your business doing?" You might know them to be in the pencil business or something, a wholesaler of pencils. It doesn't matter. This is just an example.

So, you ask them, "Hey, how is your business doing?"

And they tell you, "Ha ha ha, listen, I have been out of the pencil business for the last three months. That market is overcrowded. There's too much competition. It's like a shark tank. Everybody is eating each other alive. It just wasn't for me."

So, you're like, "Ah, I see. So, what are you doing now?"

And they tell you, "Oh, I'm in the luxury watch business now. This is the business. This is where I'm going to make my millions."

Six months later, you run into them again and ask, "Hey, how's the luxury watch business?" And it all starts over again. They tell you about how that market was overcrowded, and they tell you how they've switched to something else now, and the whole thing is just madness. They're always jumping from one thing to another, and they never stick with anything long enough to have any sort of success. It's the classic case of shiny object syndrome, and it just doesn't work.

Before you think I'm coming down hard on this type of person, I've got to tell you this. I used to be a pretender. In fact, I used to be a master pretender. And I was always busy, and I was always broke.

The third way people play the business game is they play not to lose. They don't like to take any risks. They're afraid to make big moves. Everything they do has to be calculated, recalculated and then re-recalculated. They just play defense.

Think about a soccer team. In soccer, you have 11 players on the field per team. It's 11 against 11. Now, let me ask you a question. Can you win the game if you have 11 goalkeepers?

Absolutely not. There is no way. But this is how a lot of people play the game of business. They play defense only, and they do this primarily because they lack confidence, and they are fearful. Or, even worse, they have completely lost their hunger and drive!

Maybe they've been hurt in the past, or they are afraid of losing what they already have. Or maybe they're just afraid to take it up another level. They want to be in business, but they think to themselves, "Hey, I don't want to make too much noise. I don't want to market myself too much. I don't want to express myself on social media. I don't want to come out in full color."

They have all sorts of excuses for why they're just playing defense. But if they were to go from a defensive mindset to playing a proper game, being aggressive in the marketplace by shouting who they are, what they do and how they do it, they would move from playing a defensive game to playing an attacking game. And that's when business becomes exciting.

Business is an offensive sport. When you play the business game offensively, it can take you from making small money to being rich and creating financial freedom for your family and your loved ones. This is exactly what I teach entrepreneurs how to do in my signature program for entrepreneurs - *Business Rebel Masterclass.*

What difference can this make in someone's life, switching from a defensive game to an attacking, offensive game? Well, it can make all the difference. It can take someone from earning, say, $75,000 a year to earning $500,000 a year.

As one of Europe's leading business and success coaches, I always ask my students, "How are you playing the game? Are you just playing defense? Are you aggressive? Are you a striker? Are you playing a forward role? Are you attacking?"

The fourth way people play the business game is they play to win. They want to win the game. These entrepreneurs actually wake up in the morning, and they say, "I want to win!"

This is all well and good, but here is the problem with this mindset I've discovered having been in business for many years, having taken on all of these different ways of playing the game myself.

The problem with solely wanting to win is you will end up making a deal with someone you might not even like, someone you don't even trust or want to work with. And you make this deal solely because it's going to make you money. You do it because it brings you a financial benefit or some kind of benefit at the end of the rainbow.

Because of this benefit you're expecting to gain, you become willing to compromise your values. You become willing to compromise your integrity. You become willing to compromise your sincerity. In some cases, you're even willing to compromise your honesty.

If you've ever done a deal or gotten involved in a joint venture with someone, and then lost sleep over it wondering if the person you just got involved with would actually deliver on their promises and pay you your fair, agreed upon share, then you might be in the mindset of the person who just wants to win.

Now, I'm not saying any of the stuff I've talked about in this chapter is good or bad, right or wrong. I'm telling you all of this because my intention is to make the invisible, visible for you. I just want to create awareness. I want you to be aware that there are different types of people out there doing business, and you yourself may occupy any one of these types of people doing business at a given point in time. I know I have. I've been them all at one time or another.

The key thing I want you to take away from all of this is this: you need to be aware of how you're playing the game, so you can change what needs to be changed, keep what needs to stay the same the same, and grow into the fully balanced, honest, sincere and ass-kicking entrepreneur I know you have the potential to be.

You see, the four types of people I just talked about are all the status-quo. But, if you're reading this book, you're about to discover there is a fifth way to play the game that is totally transformative and can take you to places in life you may have never dreamed possible.

It is the way of the *Rebel Entrepreneur.*

# *Rebel Actions to Take*

- Identify how you are currently playing the game of entrepreneurship and business. Be honest. Write it down.
- Think about other entrepreneurs you know. How are they playing the game? What results are they getting?
- How do you need to adjust your game plan? Do you have one?
- What pitfalls can you avoid by being aware of your mindset and your approach to business?

## _Rebel Words of Wisdom_

_"Every human being is born equal and then some become entrepreneurs."_

Arnon Barnes

# Chapter 2

# Life by Design

In the previous chapter, we talked about different ways to play the game of business. More importantly, we got you to start thinking about how *you* are playing it. This is critically important.

You need to know where you're at. Don't keep reading this book unless you've taken the time to really think about where you're at and how you're playing the game of business. Otherwise, you will just be wasting your time.

Let me say this: it doesn't matter right now whether you're doing everything completely wrong or not, you just need to be honest about where you're at. Because until you become aware of where you're at, you cannot move forward.

Your starting point does not matter. You could be in a great situation right now, or you could be in a terrible one.

Either way, you can create bigger successes, bigger wins and a bigger bank account, whatever that means for you.

To help you do that, I'm going to show you how I play the game right now. I want you to understand this is not how I've always played it, but this is how I've played the game of business for the last few years. This is how I will play the business game to the end.

I play the business game to win on my own terms and to win on my own conditions. What I mean is, I decide who I play with. I decide how I play. I decide when I play, and I decide what the rules are. And if you are currently being coached by me or have been coached by me in the past, then you know: before we even started working together, we both agreed upon and signed my code of honor.

By doing this practice with my clients, we create a safe space, and we also create a champion's environment where winning becomes simple and natural. I have had people throw cash at me and offer to pay me top dollar for coaching to help them become more profitable, strengthen their business and guide their teams. But I have had to politely turn some of these people down, because they refused to sign my code of honor.

I am very clear when it comes to this: I only want to play with players that want to add value, contribute to the process, go all-in and have fun, too. In fact, the way I evaluate a business opportunity is through three things. I'm going to give those three things to you right now.

**Number one**, does this relate in some way, shape or form to my personal mission and values? **Number two**, will I have fun? Meaning, will I like the people I would be working with? Will I enjoy being around them?

For example, I don't want to do a business deal with a person who when they call me, I see their number on my cell phone and go, "Oh, shit - can't stand this person. But I've got to answer the phone now. Ugh. Okay."

I don't want that sort of energy in my life. I don't need it. I want to enjoy my life. To enjoy my life, I must choose who I work with. I want things to be fun, and I want the people I work with to bring a certain type of excitement, exuberance and energy to play in what we're doing together.

I have absolutely no time in my life for being miserable. Though some business people seem to relish always having some problem to work out, some person to pick a fight with, I enjoy when things go smoothly. My goal is always to enjoy doing business just as much as I enjoy any other part of my life. Life is too short to be miserable or to deal with idiots.

Finally, **number three**, will the business be profitable? It must make money. There is no sense in doing business just because it makes you feel good. That's not business. That's philanthropy. In business, you're expending tons and tons of energy to reach a goal, and that end goal must always involve making money. Otherwise, you're not going to be playing the game for very long. Money is the fuel for the game. Without it, nobody could play the game at all.

Now, I have to make some clear distinctions here. Because I know you could look at those three criteria I just mentioned and think, "That all sounds pretty selfish." Or someone might take things too far and think they are always going to get things their way all the time. In business, that's simply not true.

None of this stuff I'm talking about means you don't have to do things you don't like to do. Sometimes, we all have to do things we don't necessarily like to do, like administrative stuff (something I personally dislike doing) or things that are just not very interesting to us. There are times we have to do things in our business we're not going to enjoy. That's just a fact.

What I'm really talking about here is focusing on your values, who you are, how you want to play the game, who you want to play the game with, and at what level of intensity you want to play it. That's the big distinction I want to make.

It's taken me many years to come up with the three criteria I just talked about. One of the ways I've been able to narrow down these three criteria is by looking at what makes successful people successful. Many people don't realize how straightforward this stuff is. Let me give you an example to explain what I mean.

Let's say I want you to bake me a cake. First, I tell you every ingredient you need to put in the cake, and then I give you all the instructions for making it. If you follow what I tell you to do to a T, there is no way you're not going to end up with a cake.

But let's say you decide you know better. You decide you're going to change the recipe. You're going to add something crazy like cement to the cake instead of flour. Well, if you do this, you're not going to end up with a cake. You're going to end up with something else entirely, some Frankenstein, beastly thing that doesn't taste good at all.

Hopefully you're starting to see where this is going. The same concept applies to business. Over the last decade, I have researched, dissected and analyzed the most successful people on the planet. I've studied the Oprah Winfreys. I've studied the Mark Zuckerbergs. I've studied the Elon Musks. I've studied the Donald Trumps.

What I've learned in doing this is there's an algorithm that these people are tapped into that, when dissected, creates a very clear picture of what it takes to be successful. Basically, just like the cake baking example I shared above, if you follow the algorithm (or you could call it the 'recipe'), there are only one of two things that can happen to you.

Number one, in the worst-case scenario, you will succeed. And number two, in the best-case scenario, you will succeed big time. I'm talking, like, you'll hit the jackpot. These are really the only two options.

You might be thinking, "This guy is crazy! There are so many things that could go wrong!" Well, I'll have you know, I have the pleasure of saying with confidence I am one of the craziest people on the planet. There are very few people like me out there.

What I really believe is human beings are born equal. But only a few are born entrepreneurs. If you're reading this book right now, I believe you were born to become an entrepreneur. You have a fire in your belly. You are seeking knowledge. And if you're seeking knowledge, you will find it.

Throughout this book, I'm going to unpack for you all of the different parts of the algorithm, the recipe, the keys----for success. You might have heard these things before. But my hope is, even if you have heard similar things before, this time everything will become crystal clear for you.

I'm going to give you my flavor, my twist, my distinctions, my understanding of the algorithm for success based on what I've observed. Everything I'm going to tell you about I've learned through my own business and life experience.

What I really want you to understand is I am an entrepreneur through and through. The things I'm going to tell you about in this book---these are the things you want to do to become a successful entrepreneur.

You can trust the information in this book because it all comes from someone who has been successful as an entrepreneur. I am someone who has done it. I have had success, and I continue to have success to this day. More importantly, I have experienced the wounds, the bruises, the burns, and the black eyes that come with the territory of being an entrepreneur. I've experienced the highs and the lows, the disappointments and the triumphs.

I know so many "business coaches" out there that have fancy websites and great business cards but don't know shit about real business and have never even seen a million dollars in their life; they are completely theory based. Not me.

I've done everything in business from owning a chain of retail stores and a nightclub to licensing services and products in the real estate niche, etc. I can't even give you a full list of the businesses I have been a part of in the short space I have here.

I am someone who has been there, done that, bought the t-shirt and sold it for a profit! For over a decade, I have had financial freedom. And this financial freedom gave me the gift of time I could use to study the best of the best in the business game, and now I want to share with you what I've learned.

Let's do this.

# *Rebel Actions to Take*

- Decide today how you want to design your life and business. Write down what you want---at least 40 things!
- If considering a new business venture, use the three criteria I've outlined in this chapter to evaluate it. Or, create your own three criteria to use to evaluate it, and do it.
- There is an algorithm, a formula, a recipe, for success. Allow yourself to be open to this idea. Allow yourself to be open to success beyond your wildest imagination. Remember, one insight, one "Aha!" moment can change everything for you.

## *Rebel Words of Wisdom*

*"Success doesn't come to you, you go to it."*

Arnon Barnes

# Chapter 3

# Find Your Why and Change the Game

It is true what you've heard. One of the key things I've come to understand about business, any business---be it the pencil business, shoelace business, plastic cup business, or cell phone business---literally, in any type of business, there are challenges. There are obstacles. Shit is going to hit the fan.

This is why a lot of people don't want any part of the business world. They just want to go to their jobs, collect a paycheck and live a normal life. There is nothing wrong with this. But I don't think this is what you want out of your life.

You want to do something meaningful. You want to make a difference, and you want to live the life of your dreams, not just the life everyone thinks you should live.

But everyone out there is telling you it's impossible. They're telling you only lucky people ever make it, and they are telling you there is no sense in going for your dreams because you're just going to get disappointed.

Some of the obstacles you're going to have to face are people telling you you're not good enough. Maybe you didn't finish school (like me), so you don't have a degree. Maybe you don't have any money right now. Maybe even your family is telling you you're making a stupid decision to pursue business for yourself, and you should just give up.

But I'm here to tell you today: all of these things coming at you are external forces trying to reinforce the idea that you will never be a success. But, realize this, they are *external*. They are not within you.

The real power is the force within you. It is much, much greater than the pressures of the outside world. Let me show you what I mean.

First of all, there is an algorithm for success. It does exist. It requires hard work, dedication and a lot of sweat, blood and tears. But success is available to you. You can count on it coming to you. How can I say something so bold as that? Well, for starters, you picked up this book. Meaning, you have the intention and the willingness to learn and grow.

And that's part of every successful entrepreneur's journey to the top!

In fact, if you live and work in sync with the algorithm, success is guaranteed. Another bold statement, I know. So, let me back up that statement by diving deep down into it, by really diving deep into the algorithm itself and what it requires you to do, be and act out in your life in order to get the results you want.

So, what are the key ingredients that are going to lead you to success? Let's start with number one.

One of the key things I see across the board with most successful people on the planet is every single one of them has a very clear purpose or 'why.' Successful people are very clear about what they want. They know what their purpose is, and they know why they're doing what they're doing.

You see, every single human being on this earth wakes up in the morning and thinks, "Why the fuck am I waking up this morning?" Of course, this question might be a little clouded, or it might be pushed aside by busyness or trivial concerns. But really, this question is running in the back of every single human being's mind. Why am I here? What am I supposed to do today?

Now, when you have self-awareness, you can first take notice of that question. You can begin to understand what that question means, and you can begin to answer that question of why you're here doing what you're doing and being what you're being on this planet.

You can begin to look at why you're doing what you're doing, day in and day out, week after week, month after month, year after year. In doing this, you're cultivating an incredible force within yourself. You're cultivating incredible power you're going to need to push yourself through to the point of success.

Why do you need to cultivate this power? Well, because, like I said, shit's going to hit the fan. People are going to say you're not good enough. Many, many external things are going to come against you, and they're going to try to eat away at your will to move forward with your plans. If you haven't already noticed this, just keep moving forward. This is going to happen. It happens to all of us who begin the entrepreneurial journey.

But when your 'why' and your purpose are clear and well developed, you will be able to overcome the outside forces that will inevitably come against you. You'll be able to overcome your moments of doubt, and move forward. So, the first thing you've really got to do is really clarify your 'why.'

Why are you doing what you're doing? Why do you want to be in business? What is the purpose?

For me, one of the reasons I chose to be in business is because I wanted freedom. And that was, actually, a big mistake. Because, looking back from where I'm at today, I've realized when I started out in business 25 years ago, I worked way harder than I had to when compared with how hard I would have had to work if I was just working at some job. Way harder. I can't say this enough, because I know a lot of people want the same thing I wanted---freedom, and this is just the truth a lot of people and coaches out there aren't going to tell you.

Freedom really didn't come until later. Most people though, they start a business because they want freedom. But let me tell you something: if you start a business looking for freedom, you're going to be sorely disappointed. You're going to have to sacrifice a lot in order to build momentum behind your business. You're going to have to delay freedom so much that if it's the one and only reason you started a business, you will likely flounder, and you will likely give up. It's just not a strong enough 'why' to stand on its own and get you through the tough beginning stages of starting a business, making money and becoming profitable!

When I consider my 'why' today, it looks much different. I do what I do because I really want the best for my son. I travel all over the world very often meeting with business owners and entrepreneurs, teaching and training them. But when I am in my country, in my hometown, every morning, I take my son to school.

I am one of the few fathers who show up every single day. I wake up early for my son. I even prepare his food. I get everything ready for him every morning. Because for me, putting the radio on with my four-year-old and singing happy songs with him during the drive to his school is a blessing no amount of money can buy. It's experiences like this---they are why I do what I do.

I've found in my experience with entrepreneurship things like, "Oh, I want freedom," and, "Oh, I want a million in the bank" are bullshit reasons to pursue this kind of life. They are complete bullshit. There must always be a deeper purpose. You must always have a deeper purpose. You need to be able to look within, and you need to really look at why you're doing what you're doing.

Entrepreneurship is really just a form of creative expression. For me, the gift entrepreneurship has given me is the ability to express my love towards my son. My entire team knows it doesn't matter what happens, I don't do 8AM meetings. My first meeting happens at 9AM, Monday through Friday. Nobody has access to me until 9AM after I've dropped my son off at school. That time that I have with my son---that's the gift. That's the gift of entrepreneurship for me.

That's the true gift of understanding your 'why' and your purpose. It's not some fabricated idea of wanting "freedom." In a sense, yes, I want freedom, but when you look at the core of it, the real power behind it all is in being able to have that time with my son. When obstacles and challenges show up, I am ready to meet them head on because I have a clear purpose for why I'm doing what I'm doing.

When there isn't cash flow, or something doesn't turn out the way I expect, I'm able to get this mental picture of my son, and I just say to myself, "Let's pick up the phone. Let's make magic happen. Let's hustle. Let's rock n' roll, baby. Let's kick ass!"

So, this is really the first part of the success algorithm. Everyone across the board, from the Winfreys to the Zuckerbergs, have a very clear 'why' and purpose. You really can't get where you want to go without knowing why you want to get there. Success does not come without meeting challenges head on. Having a clear 'why' will give you the strength to break through everything that tries to stand in your way on the path to realizing your dreams.

The second part of the success algorithm is goal setting. You might be thinking, "Oh, I know all about goal setting. I know how important it is, and I think about my goals all the time." Well, that may be. But there is a really important distinction I want to make about goals right now. If you really internalize it, it can change your life.

One of the things I always tell my students is this: poor people fantasize, middle-class people dream, rich people have goals, and the ultra-successful (also known as the wealthy) focus on game changers! You see, really high achievers don't just focus on goals. They're not interested in small, incremental change. They're focused on que

"What action can I take right now that is going to cc

change the game for me, my family and our bank a

This is why in my training programs I don't encourage people to just "set a goal." Just setting a goal is giving in to weak energy. A game changer opens you up to a completely different energy. Game changers are what the Beyonces, the Michael Jacksons, the Dwayne Johnsons and the Michael Jordans of this world focus on. They don't have goals; they have game changers. They focus on completely changing the game for themselves and the people they care about. They focus on doing things big.

As an entrepreneur, if you want to get to the next level, I encourage you to put your goals to the side. I'm not saying goals are bad. I'm just saying goals are low energy.

Instead, approach things from a game changer perspective, and ask yourself this question: "What is something I can do that might take me three months to a year to achieve, but would completely revolutionize my business, my lifestyle and my bank account?"

Your answer? That, my friend, is your game changer. That is what is going to completely change the game for you. Put all your eggs in that basket, and believe in your ability to make it happen. You will be amazed at how quickly it is possible to totally revolutionize your entire life when you put this way of thinking into practice.

# *Rebel Actions to Take*

- Identify your why and your purpose. Write them down.
- Ask yourself: "What is something I can do that might take me three months to a year to achieve, but would completely revolutionize my business, my lifestyle and my bank account?"
- This answer is your game changer. Focus everything you've got to this end. All ultra-successful people think and act in this way.

## *Rebel Words of Wisdom*

*"The greatest treasures on this planet, are reserved for the action takers."*

Arnon Barnes

# Chapter 4

# The Energy of Gratitude

Everything is energy. Think I'm joking? I'm not, and here's why. If you look around you, you see solid objects. But the actual science of what's going on in front of your eyes is millions and millions of tiny particles buzzing around and colliding into each other at speeds you can't even perceive in order to create the object or thing you're perceiving.

I'll say it again in case the first time didn't take for you: everything is energy. Money is energy. If you approach things with big energy, you will get big results. If you approach things with low energy, you will get low results.

Big energy equals big money. Low energy equals little money. This is a simple law of the universe. So, if your goal is to make big money, you're going to have to approach your business and entrepreneurial endeavors with big energy.

As an entrepreneur, your real job is to increase your energy levels. You see, it is very easy to approach life in an average way. Most average people wake up exhausted, and then they head into work and approach their work with a low energy, "just-get-through-the-day" mentality. I'm not saying this is bad. I'm just telling you the truth of how things really are.

You can't live this way as an entrepreneur, especially if you're just starting out. In the beginning, it requires a huge amount of energy just to build a little bit of momentum up behind the product, service or solution you're providing.

Think of it like trying to push a giant rock down from on top of a mountain. At first, you're going to have to push that rock on the flat mountaintop plateau. It's not going to want to move. It's been on top of that damn mountain for thousands, maybe even millions of years. You're going to have to really push that big rock with a lot of energy to get it to move at all.

But once you get it moving, you're eventually going to reach the edge of the mountain---where the slope gets really steep, and it's at this point that you are finally moving with the forces of the mountain and gravity at an incredibly high speed and energy rate. Look, at this point, that rock is going to move so fast, you better be careful where you've positioned it to start barreling down that mountain. Building momentum in business works just like this. It can take a lot of time and energy to really get things moving.

So, as entrepreneurs, we've got to really increase our energy levels. We need to have the energy to really get things moving. Average energy will get you practically nowhere in this game. Especially in today's competitive and volatile marketplace. But, big energy over time will get you big results. Never forget this.

The third key of the success algorithm is gratitude. This is a really big one on Oprah Winfrey's list and other high achievers' lists like her. The attitude of gratitude is the best gift you can give yourself as an entrepreneur.

Here's the key. Most entrepreneurs and business owners are always focused on what they don't have and what they lack. They're so focused on the end result that they can't see the good in their current situation.

They're always saying stuff, consciously or unconsciously, like, "Oh, until I make a million dollars a year, I won't be happy." But the truth is, you've got to be grateful for where you're at today. If you want to get to where you desire to go in the future, you must start by appreciating where you're at right now.

There's an unwritten law in the universe that says, "You cannot have more of anything until you've learned to appreciate what you've got." If you want that new car, you've got to be grateful for the car you have right now. If you want more clients or customers for your business, you've got to be grateful for the ones you have right now.

A lot of entrepreneurs operate from a mindset and energy of scarcity and lack. If you are operating from this energy, all you're going to do is create more of this energy in your life and business. So, if this is you, it's time to stop, take a deep breath, look around and appreciate everything that's around you.

I know your focus might be to have a hundred clients paying you. And I know until you get those hundred clients, you're not going to want to celebrate what's going on in your business. But that is the wrong energy to have.

If you approach what you're doing with this energy, and you act as if what's in front of you is never good enough, then you will always feel lack. Truth is, even when you get to a hundred clients, you're immediately going to want more. So, you must cultivate appreciation for all the things you've got going for you right now.

When you stop to express gratitude, you emit a very powerful energy to the universe. Like I said earlier, the best attitude you could possibly have is the attitude of gratitude. This is why every morning I wake up, and I express my gratitude. Every night when I put my son to bed, we talk about what we're grateful for.

I ask my little boy, "What are you grateful for?" And I say to him, "Daddy is so grateful for you and to be able to have this beautiful day with you." I let him know how grateful I am we are a part of each other's lives.

I am grateful for many, many things. I'm grateful for my relationships. I'm grateful for my health. I'm grateful for the clean water I get to drink each day, and the healthy, nutritious food I get to put in my body. But many people have difficulty expressing gratitude.

I do an exercise with my coaching clients where I tell them, "I want you to list in 60 seconds as many things you're grateful for as possible." So, in 60 seconds, they usually list about five to seven things. But they almost always forget about the basic things we all take for granted, like clean water to drink.

Recently, I was in Africa in the country of Tanzania. On my trip to Tanzania to climb Mount Kilimanjaro, I chose to go work in an orphanage there. The children in this orphanage have almost nothing. Seeing that first hand made me realize how much we take for granted in the Western world. These children have very little, yet they live their lives with such gratitude for everything they do have.

In the Western world, we just open the tap, and there is water to drink. But there are people who wake up every single morning and walk five to eight kilometers every day just for water. Notice I didn't even say clean water. Just water. They have to go through a whole process just to make it drinkable after that, and they do this every single day, while we have access to clean water with just the twist of a knob.

I'm not saying all this to make you feel bad. I'm saying all this to help you realize how good you've got it in a way maybe you hadn't realized before. And, really, by starting with being grateful for the most basic things you have in your life, you will find the attitude of gratitude will begin to spread to all areas of your life.

If you want more good in your life, you must start by appreciating and being grateful for the good things you've already got. This is an unspoken law of the universe, and it is a major key in the algorithm of success.

# *Rebel Actions to Take*

- Take time to fully understand that energy is everything, and everything is energy.
- Every morning for the next 30 days, take 3 minutes to write down all the things you are grateful for in your life. While writing them down, feel feelings of gratitude, and watch how magic starts to happen in your life.
- Each evening, spend time thinking about or talking about everything you're grateful for.

## <u>*Rebel Words of Wisdom*</u>

*"You can't hope, dream or meditate yourself into success, there is going to be a moment where you actually need to get up off your ass and take action. And the sooner the better"*

Arnon *Barnes*

# Chapter 5

# How to Build Confidence in Yourself

I am a huge Liverpool soccer fan, and I have been for many years. There is one thing I've discovered by watching and researching the top performing athletes on this planet, including all the players on the Liverpool soccer team. When they do something good, they all celebrate!

When somebody scores a goal, they all celebrate. When somebody makes a good pass, they all celebrate. They celebrate the action. And when they celebrate together, it makes the whole team stronger internally. They build the momentum of the game up in their favor. Even the fans can feel the excitement and energy, and they respond by cheering their team on even harder.

You see, for me, celebrating has what I call a "lock on" effect. People always ask me questions like, "What is the benefit of celebrating? Arnon, why do you believe celebrating is so important?"

And I tell them, "Well, it's important for many reasons. But one of the key reasons celebrating is important is because when you celebrate, you create very powerful internal energy."

What is this powerful internal energy? You've no doubt heard of it before. It's called confidence. From my experience, I can tell you the most confident people on the planet are often the wealthiest, the happiest, and the most successful. Confidence really is a key element for success. You literally need it if you want to be a success.

So, how do you increase your confidence? By celebrating! Celebrate your wins. Celebrate the contracts you get. Celebrate the new clients you bring on board. Celebrate the meetings you take part in. Celebrate the money coming in to your bank account.

When you celebrate the little things, you attract the bigger things. Most people say, "Oh, well, yeah… It's just a small win. I'm not going to celebrate such a small win." But listen, if you can't celebrate the small wins, there's no way you're ever going to get to celebrate the big wins.

You've got to build the muscle of celebration before you can celebrate the big wins. It's just like training for a sport. You don't go into the gym and pack on the big weights on your first day out. You go in, and you gradually build up your muscles so that later they will serve you in whatever big competition you're training for.

If I told you, "Listen, tomorrow morning at 6AM, you need to wake up, and you need to run a marathon."

Some of you reading this might be like, "Let's rock n' roll." But others of you probably have a look of horror on your face because you're not in mental, emotional or physical shape to do such a thing. Because you haven't been training yourself for that sort of thing. You don't have the muscles needed to achieve it.

But if I said, "Tomorrow morning at 6AM, I want you to run a kilometer or two, and the next day add one more to whatever you did," then you'd probably be willing to at least try it. You'd know you could probably do it, even if it was really hard, and you could see how you are doing this would build a pattern that would eventually lead to you being ready to run a marathon if I told you to.

It's the same thing with success, celebrating and increasing your confidence. If you want to have success in your life, you've got to learn to celebrate the small wins. Not only does doing this give you more confidence, it also allows you to start acknowledging your inner child---meaning, it allows you to actually have fun with what you're doing in life.

If you're not having fun with what you're doing, you will probably start to self-sabotage your own success without even knowing why. If you forget to celebrate a new contract, your first client or that first invoice being paid, you're going to slowly deteriorate and eventually lose your passion for what you're doing. Awakening that inner child who likes to have fun and celebrate every success is absolutely key for long-term success and enjoyment of the entrepreneurial journey.

Every great business starts with its first win and a celebration of success. An exercise I have everyone do at my events is I have everyone write down a list of successes they've had in their life, the ones they are directly responsible for. This could be a thing like having the persistence to finish school, or even something simple like having the discipline to go to the gym in the morning.

Some people say things like, "My success today was waking up and getting out of bed." Remember, everyone is at a different place in life, some very low and some very high. It doesn't matter where you're at right now. You can build from there to get to where you want to go.

Anyway, I then say to them, "Okay, are you guys willing to play with me? Put your notebooks down, stand up and close your eyes. Visualize the successes you just wrote down." I let them visualize these successes for about 30 seconds, and then I say to them, "Make those images bright. Make them big. Make them colorful in your mind."

They do this with their eyes closed. Then I say, "When you have the images big and vibrant in your mind, just gently put a smile on your face so I know you're connected to that energy and space of success you're seeing in your mind right now. Keep your eyes closed."

Once I see everyone smiling and connected, I say, "Okay, keep your eyes closed. I'm going to count to three, and when I get to three, I want you to celebrate your successes, whatever they are, like your team has just won the Football World Cup. I want you to celebrate like crazy!"

An awesome thing happens when I get to three. The whole room goes wild. People start jumping up and down, high-fiving each other and yelling at the top of their lungs. It's really quite an incredible sight to see from my point of view on the stage.

Then, as people start to settle down, I ask the whole audience a very direct question. I ask, "So, now, are you feeling stronger or weaker?"

Everybody yells, "Stronger!"

I ask, "Are you feeling more confident or less confident?"

Everybody yells, "More confident!"

I ask, "Are you feeling powerful, or are you feeling weak?"

Everybody yells, "Powerful!"

Now, the next part is where this whole concept really solidifies for the audience. I tell them, "Great! Now, if you celebrate every day like you just did, when the shit hits the fan, you will be able to tap into this energy you feel pulsing through you right now." I ask them, "Do you believe, right now, that you have the internal power to overcome anything?"

Everybody in the audience yells, "Yes!" And they walk away from this experience with a huge insight. I get letters all the time from people telling me how they began celebrating their wins after attending one of my events and how this simple practice has created magic in their lives.

So, I encourage all of you reading this right now to start acknowledging and celebrating your wins. Celebrate your successes. It can be as simple as looking at yourself in the mirror, patting yourself on the back and saying, "I'm proud of you. Good job. You did well." It's so simple, but not enough people do this.

Fair warning: when you don't do this, things start to go in the opposite direction. Your thoughts start to get very cloudy, and you start to say things to yourself like, "You're not good enough. You haven't accomplished enough, You don't deserve more success."

*SO TRUE!*

49

Those types of thoughts are nothing but complete bullshit. I can guarantee you have something in your life worth celebrating right now. If you are really hard pressed to think of something, just turn on your TV. Watch a sports game, and look at how the players celebrate when something good happens. You'll get a masterclass on how to celebrate a win, and you can carry that energy with you into your own life, make it your own.

Celebrate the little wins now, and you will get to celebrate the big wins later on!

# *Rebel Actions to Take*

- Write down a list of successes you've had in your life.
- Close your eyes, and visualize these successes. Make them very big, vibrant and colorful in your imagination
- Open your eyes, and celebrate like mad!
- Take note of the energy this creates around you. Do you feel confident? Do you feel capable? Do you feel powerful?
- Practice this as much as possible. It will build up your confidence. Guaranteed!

A "DAILY DO"

## *Rebel Words of Wisdom*

"The universe rewards focused actions, not scattered thoughts."

Arnon Barnes

# Chapter 6

# The Power of Belief

Hopefully, at this point in the book, you are really seeing how powerful the energy we create around ourselves is. You are beginning to see how powerful confidence can be when it comes to achieving what you want to achieve in life.

Now, I want to add to the conversation we've been having about confidence. You see, there is an aftereffect of being confident; that is, being confident creates belief.

A few years ago, there was a soccer club that won the English Premier League. At the start of the Premier League season, the bookies gave them a 1 in 5,000 shot at winning the League. In other words, if you bet ten dollars on them winning the League, and they did, you would get $50,000.

And guess what? They did it. They won the English Premier League.

This club was called Leicester City Football Club. At the time, their manager was an Italian gentleman named Claudio Ranieri. When they won the Premier League, I became very curious about the team, and I wanted to understand what their magic ingredient or ingredients were that led to their success.

After watching a bunch of interviews with their coach, Ranieri, I noticed there was one word that kept popping up in every single interview. There was one key phrase he kept saying over and over, and it was, "These lads, these boys, they have belief."

Belief. Belief. Belief. Belief. Belief. There it is, the secret ingredient to success that brought a true underdog to the top of the English Premier League. They were given a 1 in 5,000 shot at winning, but clearly that prediction did not shake their belief in themselves that they could do it.

Now, knowing that belief is so powerful, how do we go about cultivating it in our own lives? Well, I believe that celebrating creates confidence, and I will now take that a step further and say that confidence creates internal belief. This is another part of the success algorithm that is prevalent across the board.

The Oprah Winfreys, the Donald Trumps, the Mark Zuckerbergs, the Richard Bransons---all of these people have incredibly strong belief in themselves, who they are and what they are capable of. This is something super important that is often forgotten.

People just don't think about how important this concept is. It's almost like a forgotten language, but it is very, very powerful. You know, there is that extremely famous quote from Henry Ford that says something to the effect of, "Whether you think you can, or think you can't, either way, you're right."

The problem with everyone knowing this quote is that it's become a cliché. Many people hear this, and they think one of two things. They think, "Oh, that's obvious," and then they completely forget what the quote is actually getting at.

Or they hear this quote and think, "No way, that's not even true. Henry Ford was lucky, and he achieved what he did because he had a freakish amount of luck. That's all there is to it."

But, let's take a moment, and let's really get inside this frame of mind where belief is given proper consideration. Do you really, honestly think belief is not powerful? Do you think you can walk around in your daily life believing you are a screw-up, no-good-for-nothing person, and at the same time run the wildly successful and profitable business of your dreams?

You see, it only takes answering a few questions to realize the incredibly strong link between what we believe about ourselves and the outcomes we get to experience in life. If you believe you can do it, you can. If you believe you can't do it, you can't. It really is that simple.

So, remember, the aftereffect of confidence is belief. You become confident by celebrating the little successes and the big successes. The more you live in the energy of confidence, the greater your belief in yourself will grow.

Most people spend way too much time doubting themselves, and they call this "being realistic." Sure, yeah, I guess this is true, because what you believe about yourself is going to end up creating your reality in some way.

If you believe you don't have what it takes, you're not going to have what it takes. If you believe you do have what it takes, you're going to have what it takes. This is super important, and that's why I'm hammering it into you right here, right now. In my 8-week signature coaching program titled *Super Action*, I give my clients a simple, and very effective two-part exercise that radically changes their belief system about themselves and their success in a positive, empowering way.

Now, you've probably heard on the news or somewhere about that statistic about how most businesses fail. But guess what? You now know the truth. You now know the secret ingredient nobody really talks about in the media, unless you know where to look.

You know the story of the Leicester City Football Club who were given 1 in 5000 odds from everyone around them of winning the English Premier League. And you know exactly how they pulled it off. You know how they won. They had a belief that they could do it.

Now, what do you believe you can do?

# *Rebel Actions to Take*

- The aftereffect of confidence is belief. You become confident by celebrating all of your successes. What success can you celebrate today that will lead you on the path to increased confidence and belief in yourself?

- What belief do you have about yourself and your capabilities right now? Write it down. Be honest, even if it isn't flattering.

- What belief do you want to have? Write it down. Affirm it to yourself daily, and take the actions required to build your confidence.

## ***Rebel Words of Wisdom***

*"The best way to help the poor, is not to become one of them."*

Arnon Barnes

# Chapter 7

# Not Selling – Closing!

We've been looking at the way the most successful people on the planet approach life and business. Hopefully you've been completing the action steps at the end of each chapter as well. If not, go back and start doing them. They really will help you get the results you want. Now, I want to give you another very important part of the success puzzle, and that is closing.

You see, a lot of people focus on selling. But I don't want the people who study with me to just go out and "sell" more. If that were really to become their focus, I would just be making my students more and more busy with nothing to show for it. What I want my students to do is close more. I'm not into selling. I'm into closing because closing is a higher and stronger energy.

In one of my advanced, live trainings for entrepreneurs, I put all of my students through a very powerful, very insightful process of experiential learning, and I teach them how to close. By the time they have completed the process and are on their way home from the event, they have developed a sense of invincibility when it comes to sales and closing.

It's almost like they've become bullet proof by having gone through my process. It's a game-changer! In fact, I build up so much muscle for them in the arena of closing, that by the time we are done and dusted, they have almost no resistance to selling, when before, just the word "selling" might have made them crumble like superman coming into contact with kryptonite.

Most people hear the word "selling," and they go into shock. Their minds immediately create a picture of a sleazy, dishonest used car salesman or something, somebody who is just out to make a buck at the expense of unsuspecting strangers. In fact, car salesmen are the number two most disliked professionals in the world, right behind politicians. That tells you something right there.

But the truth is selling is the lifeblood of any business. Now, again, I don't like to talk about just selling. I like to talk about closing. The act of closing is much more important than the act of selling. Closing means the job got done, and you've thrown some wood on the fire. Selling just means you wandered around in the woods looking for some sticks to burn. That's it. Plus, closing is a stronger energy than simply selling. Whilst most people are looking to hire 'salesmen', I am looking for closers, ninjas, freakin' assasins! My experience tells me, that everybody wants "big rewards."

Everybody wants a big fire, but nobody wants to put wood into the fire. Let me explain what I mean. Everybody wants to live a better lifestyle, but they're not willing to do the real work of putting energy into making that happen for themselves. They're alright with wandering around looking for sticks, but they never grab that big hunk of wood and throw it into the fire.

My experience is if you want a better lifestyle, you've got to increase your income. And if you want to increase your income, you need to be closing. Not "selling." Closing. Everybody wants a better lifestyle, but nobody wants to close. To me, that's absurd.

Almost every entrepreneur knows and has talked about Steve Jobs at one point or another. And when people talk about Steve Jobs, they say stuff like, "He was a visionary, a leader and an innovator." But do you know what they forget to say about him?

He was a closer. He was so good at closing that today, even though he's dead, when Apple launches a new product, there are huge lines of people sleeping in tents outside the doors of Apple stores waiting for that product to come out so they can be the first ones to buy it.

You can see from this example that Steve Jobs knew exactly how to present Apple products in a way that made people obsessed with buying them. And it wasn't just products he sold. He knew how to close business deals and how to get the people he needed to join his team.

When he wanted Pepsi's CEO to come work for him at Apple, he closed him with the line, "Do you want to sell sugar water for the rest of your life, or do you want to come with me and change the world?"

This is powerful, powerful stuff. But people don't talk about it. They don't call Steve Jobs a closer. But without him being a closer, Apple simply wouldn't exist. Steve Jobs could have been the most visionary leader and innovator the world has ever seen, but if Apple's products didn't sell, that wouldn't have mattered.

The same is true for you and your business. You may have incredible skills, vision, talent, ability or leadership, but if you're not closing, you're not going to get very far. Without wood for the fire, the fire doesn't exist. End of story.

If you want to become a successful entrepreneur. Than you need to be able to close. If you don't like closing, then that's probably the main reason your bank account is empty!

# *Rebel Actions to Take*

- Take a moment and think about what comes to mind when I say the words "selling" and "sales."
- If you've built a negative picture of these things up in your mind, realize that selling is the lifeblood of any business. Without sales, there is no business.
- Reframe your idea of selling into the idea of "closing." Steve Jobs was a closer. Envision yourself as a closer instead of a sales person. Feel the difference this can make in your attitude towards this critical part of any business.
- Remember, there is nothing more powerful in a closing situation than telling the truth.

## _Rebel Words of Wisdom_

_"The level of your commitment to your business will equal the size of your bank account._

_BIG commitment = BIG money._

_Mediocre commitment = Mediocre money."_

Arnon Barnes

# Chapter 8

# Negotiate Win-Win-Wins

The next key to success I've observed that all the most successful people on the planet have is the ability to negotiate. The wealthiest and best performing entrepreneurs on planet earth are great negotiators.

First of all, a lot of people have this idea in their head that negotiating is dirty. They don't like it. They think it's a bad thing to do. They think it's not classy, and they think it's just being picky and not being grateful for what's offered to you and all of that B.S. But this is simply not true.

What negotiating really is, is creating a win-win situation. What I mean by this is that the person I'm negotiating with wins and I win too, simple. Most importantly you really can learn how to negotiate with style and class. It doesn't have to be some sleazy thing where you're just trying to get something for nothing.

I remember years ago, early on in one of my relationships, we'd go into a store, and when we found something we wanted to buy, I would start to negotiate on the price with the salesperson. My girlfriend didn't want to be anywhere near me when I was doing this at first.

But, eventually, she came to understand that negotiating is an important part of life, and it is a very important part of any successful business. In time, she became an exceptionally good negotiator. I must say that having a beautiful face, beautiful hair and being able to wear a beautiful dress does sometimes help in negotiations.

But, nonetheless, the reason why negotiating and learning to negotiate is so important is because everything you want in your life is currently owned by somebody else. Think about this for a moment. We're not living in the midst of the Industrial Revolution anymore. It's not like many of you reading this are out there searching for untapped natural resources like gold or copper or any type of raw material that's just found in the earth.

In our modern era, the things you want in your life are products and services other people have created and own. You're going to have to go through the proper channels of acquiring these things. And those proper channels are always going to be people you're going to need to negotiate with.

There's an acronym I often teach my students: BATNA---this stands for Best Alternative To [a] Negotiated Agreement. This concept comes from a great book called *Getting to Yes:* written by Roger Fisher and William Ury.

In this book, the authors say, "Know your BATNA." In other words, when you go into a negotiation, you need to know where your bottom line is. For example, if you're selling something, and you're speaking to a potential buyer, you need to know how low you can go on price to meet the potential buyer's needs and still be able to consider the agreement successful, meaning, worth doing the deal for you, too.

You don't want to go into a negotiation blind. You have to set a line somewhere, and then skillfully maneuver your prospect through the negotiation process so you can create a win-win situation for both of you.

When someone comes to you and says, "I need a better discount than this," or "I need a better price on this," you've got to know where your bottom line is, or you will hold no power in the negotiation process.

One of the most powerful things you can say as the seller is, "Listen, I can't discount this thing any more than I already have. This is the offer. You can take it or leave it." If the prospective buyer really wants what you're selling, they'll find the money you're asking for.

If you're in the role of the buyer in a negotiation, one of the most powerful things you can say is, "Listen, I have no more money to give you." You want to walk away from the negotiation process with the feeling that you have won on your own terms and conditions. If everything is done properly, with class and with style, the person you're negotiating with should walk away feeling this way, too.

So, you see, there is really nothing sleazy, weird or snobbish about negotiating. It is just a normal process we all have to go through in order to acquire the products and services we want and need. When done properly, everyone wins.

It is a very important part of business and life. And it can even be a very fun part of business if you know how to view it in the right way.

In my signature program *Business Rebel Masterclass*, I teach a few incredibly powerful negotiation tactics that will blow your mind. I would love to share them with you here, but it would take me the rest of this book to do it, and putting you through the experience in my masterclass will serve you much better!

*IS THIS STILL OFFERED?*

# *Rebel Actions to Take*

- Think about how you view the negotiation process. Do you see how it is good for everyone involved, or do you view it as a process in which one person gets the short end of the stick?
- Practice negotiating for something small. Ask someone if you can buy something small of theirs which you like. Practice negotiating a fair price on the item that makes you both walk away feeling satisfied.

## _Rebel Words of Wisdom_

_"Some entrepreneurs prefer to go through the fire of life on their own, instead of asking for help. As an entrepreneur pride and ego is the most expensive thing you can own._

_Get a coach!"_

Arnon Barnes

# Chapter 9

# Vision and Focus

In this day and age, it is possible to outsource and delegate almost every single part of a business. You can outsource your marketing. You can outsource your sales. You can outsource your delivery. You can outsource your accounting. You can delegate your administration. You can even outsource your product.

But, as the leader of an organization, there is one thing you can never, ever outsource. That is the vision.

This is why as an entrepreneur, business owner or leader of your tribe, you need to be very clear about your vision. If you need an example to follow, look at Bill Gates. He had an extremely clear vision for what he wanted to accomplish with Microsoft. What was the vision Bill Gates had that made him the richest person currently on the planet, one of the most financially successful people that has ever lived in all of history, and the biggest philanthropist in all of history? What was that vision?

Well, it was very simple, and it was very powerful. His vision was to put a computer in every household. That was the vision he held onto. With this vision, he built a monstrously successful computer company called Microsoft. It's a household name. That's the kind of power a vision can bring to the world, and it's the kind of power you want behind everything you do.

As an entrepreneur, you need to hold on to your vision for your company. It is not something that can be outsourced. Hold on to it, and work towards it with all that you've got. Make it something big. Life is too short to just make small things happen. Make your vision big, look at the world from a 30,000-foot view, and then come back down to earth, get to work and take the smaller steps needed to get to the top of that mountain you want to climb.

There's just one trap you need to look out for when you start conjuring up a really big vision of what you want to do. This actually comes up quite a lot in the meetings I have with different entrepreneurs I coach.

What happens is they come to me, and they say something like, "Well, I've got this business opportunity here, and I've got this business opportunity over there. Well, see, I'm really the owner and operator of like five businesses, and what do you think? Should I quit this business? Should I start a new business? What should I do?"

My response is always the same. I say, "Look, to figure out what you should do, you don't need my opinion or anyone else's opinion. Let's just look at the facts of the matter. Let's look at successful people you want to be like, and let's see what they've done to get their success."

Oprah Winfrey---where did she make all of her money? Media. Bill Gates---where did he make all of his money? Software. Mark Zuckerberg---where did he make all of his money? Facebook. Donald Trump---where did he make all of his money? Real estate.

In other words, these really high achievers made all of their money in one industry before they started getting involved in all kinds of other industries. So, as an entrepreneur, yes, you want to have a huge vision that encompasses all the ways you want to change the world. But you also must have a focus. You must stick with one thing long enough to really begin to see the fruits of your labor there, in that one specific area, before you start branching out into a million other things trying to catch a lucky break.

Focus is extremely powerful, and a lot of people know this if they were to really think about it, but they don't put it into practice when it comes to their financial and business life.

So many people are suffering from "shiny object syndrome". They see something new, and they think, "Oh, that looks like a great opportunity! It looks easy!" And then they end up wasting their time doing like five things half assed. Not because they're lazy, but because a person simply can't do five different things in a non-half-assed way. One person simply doesn't have the time or energy required for doing that many things well. I mean to a level of mastery. It's impossible.

But focus is a superpower I encourage every entrepreneur to adopt and develop. Whether you're just starting your business---whether you're building a team or you already have a team, you need to focus.

Huge power comes from the ability to be focused. It's hard enough to take one business to the 10 million dollar or 100 million dollar mark. Why would you ever try to take five businesses that far? The bottom line is this: there are very few people who can manage this many successful businesses. Something is going to fall by the wayside with this approach.

Look, if you're a serial entrepreneur, and that kind of thing really just lights your fire and that's what you think you've been designed to do, then, by all means, go for it. But, speaking from my experience, there are very few Richard Branson's out there with hundreds of businesses. For most of us, the power of focus is going to take us so much farther than spreading ourselves thin trying to make five businesses soar to the heavens.

So, what you really want to do is focus on one company, one business, and let it fly. Let it soar. Make it the best it can possibly be. Squeeze every last drop of juice out of it. You will be amazed how with having just one focus and by being fully involved with just one business, you can experience many, many things and achieve great success. You will have a very rich experience, and you will reach the point of success much, much faster than if you tried to grow even two businesses at once.

Focus is key. Without it, you will spread yourself too thin, not be able to keep up with demands, and you will likely not have the success you aim to achieve. I'll say it again: focus on doing one thing great, and everything else, your grand vision, will fall into place.

# *Rebel Actions to Take*

- Get very clear on your vision. Hold onto it at all costs. This is the one thing that cannot be outsourced. Make it huge, make it big and bright, then work on the small things that need to be done each day to bring your vision into reality.

- Remember the power of focus. Every successful person has gained their success by focusing on one main area. Most likely, this is the path you must take to get there as well. Cut out the extra stuff today.

WHAT BENEFIT TO ANYONE DOES END PROVIDE?
- PROMISE?
↗ TANGIBLE
OTHER THAN MERCH
- BELIEF IN GOAL!
- HOW DO I SELL THAT??

## <u>Rebel Words of Wisdom</u>

*"The distance between you, success and the lifestyle you desire, is the distance between your left ear and your right ear."*

Arnon Barnes

# Chapter 10

# The Power of a Championship Team

Years ago, I used to proclaim I was a self-made man. You know, I never had a rich daddy or rich mommy that gave me millions to start a business or something. Nobody ever gave me any kind of money. Daddy never came to me and said, "Oh, son, here's a million dollars. Go make big things happen." That was never my life. Nobody ever did anything like this for me.

So, yeah, I claimed to be a self-made man. But today, I'm wiser than to say that. I'm smarter, and I've realized there is really no such thing as a self-made man or woman. This whole concept of a person who has just carved everything out on their own and done everything on their own doesn't exist in reality.

Today, I understand the only reason I'm successful is because I've always had people around me. I've always had a team around me. This is really a major key to success. Anything that has ever been created and become great on this planet was created by a team of people working together.

Yeah, there might have been a leader of that team. Yeah, there was probably someone who served as the visionary or the innovator that began the whole process of creation for everyone. But anything great that was ever accomplished on this planet was accomplished by a team.

This is why as an entrepreneur you need to build a team. But not just any team. You need to build a championship team. I always say just because you have people coming into your office, working under one roof and collecting a paycheck from the same company, doesn't mean those people are a team. You might just have a group of individuals who happen to congregate in the same place every week, not a team.

Now, when I build a team, I always look and make sure the people I invite to join my team understand this principle: mission always comes first, the team comes second and the individual comes third. With most businesses, it's the other way around. People go to work, and they put themselves first, the team second and the mission of the company third. But things just don't work the best when the structure of a company is set up to be like this.

I have worked with, studied and researched some of the most successful people on the planet, and the most successful entrepreneurs and business owners I know are successful because they have a championship team that is built on the idea of mission first, team second and individual third.

In order to create a championship team, one of the things I've learned over the years from many teachers who have helped me on my path is the importance of having and creating what I call a code of honor for the team. A code of honor defines how your team as a unit and tribe are going to play the game together. What values do you share? What are the most important things your team must see eye to eye on as you go forward together?

I spent three years serving as a soldier in the Israeli Defense Force (IDF). It's probably one of the toughest armies in the world because members are required to defend their country. If you live in Israel, you go to the army. It's not a choice. It doesn't matter if you're male or female, you go to the army. When you turn 18 years old, you go to the army.

Now, when I was in the IDF, I was given a very strict code of honor to follow: never abandon a soldier in need;

never leave your team member; nobody gets left behind. There are certain principles we were made to follow to keep ourselves and everyone around us safe. This is really what having a code of honor is all about. It protects the team as a unit, and it makes sure the team is effective and can get the job done without casualties.

If you're building a team without a code of honor, you probably aren't really creating a team. All you are building is a group of individuals who come into work Monday through Friday, do their 9 to 5 and then go home. And they all do this together until they're 65, say thank you, leave and never come back. They're not invested in what they're doing any more than the absolute bare minimum necessary to collect a paycheck.

A true team must have a shared vision. They are working together towards a goal, a mission. They know where their loyalties lie. You see, there is no such thing as a self-made man or woman. We all depend on each other much more than we think.

When you have the right team in place, and you have a code of honor you know all the members of the team are going to follow, you can truly put your trust in them. You don't have to grind out your day to day, feeling like you're forcing other people around you to do your bidding.

You know your brother or sister is there for you, you know they've got your back when challenges come up, and you know that with them, your business is going to soar to heights you never even imagined. This is the power of a championship team.

# *Rebel Action to Take*

- What is your business's code of honor? Take time to think about this, and write it down.
- If you're a solo entrepreneur, or working with contractors , what is your personal code of honor? How do you want to present yourself as a business man or woman? What are your values? What values do you want your future team to have? Write your top 10 points down, embrace them and live by them; watch how magic happens in your business when you implement a code of honor. This is exactly what I teach in my Business Rebel Masterclass. For more information on my event calendar visit www.businessrebelmasterclass.com and sign up for this 2 day's of game-changing material.

## _Rebel Words of Wisdom_

_"Your success will not be determined by what you know, not by who you know, it will be determined by who knows you."_

Arnon Barnes

# Chapter 11

# Comfort Zones and Branding

---

You might have heard the cheesy cliché that says, "All the magic happens outside of your comfort zone." It's easy to pass this one off as just another thing people say. Believe me, I know people say a lot of stupid things that don't apply to real life, but this is not one of those things. This is for real. Sometimes clichés are cliché for a good reason. I believe this is one of those instances.

You see, successful people---the really high achievers we've been talking about throughout this entire book---they are all aware of their comfort zones. But more importantly, they are also constantly trying to push their boundaries.

Average people like to stay in one place. In fact, one of the main goals in their lives is just to remain comfortable. To get the house, the car, the retirement account, and then just relax on the beach until they die.

But the high achievers don't think like this. When these people get pushed outside of their comfort zones, they welcome the opportunity. They see the chance to get outside of the comfort zone as an opportunity for themselves to grow.

Let's consider what would happen if this wasn't the case. Imagine if Michael Jackson had been given the opportunity to go out on stage in front of thousands of people for the first time, and his response was, "Oh, no, I don't think I can do that. I've never done that before. That's outside of my comfort zone. Sorry, not going to do it." If this was his response, he would be robbing the world of his gift and talents. He would literally be acting as a thief.

As an entrepreneur and business owner, you are in the same situation. You need to know where you're at, your comfort zone. But you also have to be willing to push through it and expand it.

This is why when I get called to go help companies all over the world, the first thing I do before I start doing anything with them is I meet the owner. I meet the leader. I want to shake their hand, look them in the eye and talk with them. Because I understand that an organization will never grow bigger than its leader.

If there is a big leader in charge of the company, then the company has big potential, big opportunities and will likely get big results. If there is a small leader in charge of the company, then the company has small potential, small opportunities and will likely get small results.

In order to help an organization to really grow, when I work with companies, I work on developing and growing the leader. You see, it doesn't matter if you're the biggest company in the world with the most incredible amount of talented people on staff, if your leadership is small-minded and underdeveloped, the company itself is not going to do very well.

You as an entrepreneur reading this book are shooting for or are in this situation. You are the leader of your company, whether it's just you and a few contractors right now, or if it's you and 1,000 people on staff.

In my work, I focus on really developing leaders and showing them what it takes to run a successful business. Because without strong, capable and confident leaders, organizations crumble.

Another key for success is if you want to create a memorable product or service, and move out of obscurity, you have to build a brand. You need to build a brand people can relate to. You've got to create a story of who you are, what you do, why you do what you do, and how you do it.

This is harder to do today than ever before. Why? Because in today's marketplace, it is easy to call yourself a therapist, a yoga teacher, a trainer or a coach. It is easy in today's world to label yourself anything you want. No one can really stop you, even if you have no clue what you're doing.

Understand this: the internet broke down all the barriers. I can pick up the phone right now, call my assistant, and I can say, "I need a new website built and a new business card printed. I want you to put on there that I'm a healer, coach and personal trainer." It really doesn't matter. I can call myself almost anything I want. I could even tell my assistant, "Oh, yeah, I'm also a distributor of luxury watches. Put that on there, too."

Bottom line is, it would cost me about $500 to create a simple website, and maybe another $30 to print a hundred business cards. I could be up and running in less than a week! That would be the total investment for me to become known as any of the things I mentioned or all of the above. This is just an example, but you get what I mean.

I say all of this for a reason. I want you to know how easy it is in today's world for somebody to stand up. But it is very, very difficult for somebody to stand out. This is why branding is so important. It is so powerful.

A lot of people say, "Oh, you know, it's not what you know, it's who you know." But that's bullshit. It's not what you know, and it's not who you know. It is who knows you. And you build this recognition through branding.

You know, I've met so many people who think they can pray themselves into success. They think they can meditate themselves into financial freedom. They think they can "om" themselves into business and money success. And the truth is if you think you can sing kumbaya and make money fall from the heavens, it's better if you just go back to your cave.

One of the single most important factors that will determine your success is your ability to take massive action. Your willingness to literally stop, put your ego aside and say, "Fuck it. I might look stupid, but I'm going to do it anyway."

Remember, the greatest treasures on this planet are reserved for the action takers. You can't hope yourself into wealth. At some point in time, you're going to have to get up off your ass and take massive, decisive action. Remember, the universe rewards actions, not thoughts.

When you look across the board at the most successful and wealthiest people on the planet, you see they are people who are massive freaking action takers. It's really important to look at these people and ask, "How did they do it? What are the steps? What methods did they use?"

You see, like I said earlier in this book, over 90 percent of millionaires made their money from something called business. Now, you know that this is how they did it. So, don't you think it's a good idea to get involved in the game of business, and take massive, focused action? This is pretty obvious, right?

But still a lot of people say, "Oh, business is not for me. It's just not me." And listen, if business is not for you, that's fine. But what chance do you have then to create wealth in your life?

I'm not saying you won't win the lottery. I'm not saying your Uncle Joe isn't going to die and leave you $20 million. These are possibilities, however slim. But what I'm really saying is 90% of the wealthiest people on the planet got to where they are through business. It's really simple. It's so simple, it needs to be said more than once because so many people think there is no path to wealth for the average person. And that's just not true. There is a path.

It's called business. I am living proof that you can come from nothing: I began with no money, no finished college program, no degree or fancy certificate hanging on my wall. But with focus, massive action and commitment to the business game, a path opened up for me.

This is why I consider myself a *Rebel Entrepreneur,* and this is why I am inviting you to be one as well. Because when the doors are locked, we come through the window. If the windows are shut tight, we come down the chimney. No chimney? We kick the front door down!

It doesn't matter what kind of life you come from. In business, if you want it bad enough, you can find a way to get it. And I'm here to help you do it.

# *Rebel Actions to Take*

- What does your comfort zone look like? Are you willing to break through it to get to the gold on the other side? Are you willing to say, "Fuck it, I don't care how stupid I look. I'm doing this thing," or not?

- How does your business stand out? Do you have a brand people can connect with, know and like? Do people know what you do, how you do it and why you do it? Do they know your story?

- Are you willing to take massive action? What is one big move you can make today that might change the course of your business and life forever?

## *Rebel Words of Wisdom*

*"Everybody wants more happiness, more money and better relationships, everybody wants the fire, very few people are willing to put in the wood to create it."*

Arnon Barnes

# Chapter 12

# The Game of Business

In the game of business, it's very important to know what not to do, but it's also equally important to know what to do. So, if you want to amass true wealth, and you're an entrepreneur who is reading this right now, I honor you.

There are all different ways you can play the game of business, as mentioned earlier in this book. And there are different understandings people have about what it means to build a business. But if you're an entrepreneur reading this book right now, you've probably got some skin in the game. You're a person who has decided they don't want to just play by the rules and live the life everyone else says they should.

You're a rebel. You want something better, something more. You want your life to be fulfilling on your own terms. You are the *Rebel Entrepreneur* this book was titled and made for. You have a strong energy inside you that is unshakable in the face of opposition. It's called confidence. And you believe in yourself. You believe you can achieve the success you want, and you will do it.

There's a book written by Robert T. Kiyosaki, author of the notoriously famous *Rich Dad, Poor Dad* called *The Cash Flow Quadrant.* In this book, Kiyosaki gives a diagram that explains different types of people and how they sustain themselves. Basically, how they make money and earn their keep in life.

On the top left side of the diagram, there's the employee. Underneath that, on the same side, there is the self-employed. On the top right side of the diagram, there's the business owner. And underneath that is the investor.

Now, here's the question for you. Where do you want to play? Do you want to be on the left side or on the right side? Do you want to be an employee or be self-employed? Do you want to be the business owner or the investor?

If you're reading this book right now, it's because you probably want to be the business owner or the investor. I'm just going to assume that going forward from here.

So, you want to be the business owner or the investor, right? But you've got to start somewhere, and most people start out as an employee. Here's how this journey often goes for people. This is how most people go from being an employee to becoming self-employed and starting their own business. This is what happens a lot of the time.

You start out, and you're an employee. You wake up one day, and you go to your job, and your boss says to you, "Listen, we have a strategy. We have something we need you to do."

You look at what they want you to do, and you say, "Okay, but I don't think this is going to work. This strategy just doesn't feel right. There's something off about it."

And your boss tells you, "Yeah, but this is what the big boys at the head office want us to execute on. So, get this stuff done."

So, being an employee, when your boss tells you to jump, you ask, "How high?" You start executing, but as you're working through, you see the plans are not going to work. But you continue. You continue to work. You do it week after week, month after month, and then after six months, you deliver the project, and they look at the results.

And they say, "Shit, this doesn't work. This isn't good."

All the while you're thinking, "Fuck, I knew it. I knew it. I saw this from day one, but they didn't want to listen to me. They didn't want to take my feedback. I told them it wasn't going to work."

So, you go back to your desk in your grey, dark cubicle that has no windows near it, and you get back to work. Then, 12 months later, your boss comes back to you and says, "Listen, we know how to make this work now. Here's the project again."

But you look at it this time and say, "Dude, we've tried this. It's not going to work. It doesn't fit the company. It's not suitable for our products," etc.

But your boss says, "Listen, the big boys at HQ want you to do this. So, you know, do it."

And you've got to eat. You've got to keep getting your paycheck every month. You want that security, so you execute on the project. Six months later, when it's all done, you're sitting in another meeting, and everyone is saying, "Well, this didn't work. We didn't get the results we wanted."

All the while, you're sitting there thinking, "What the fuck am I doing here? These guys are schmucks. They don't know what they're doing. I could do better. But I don't own the company. I'm just an employee. What if I started my own business? You know what? That's exactly what I'm going to do."

Now, speaking from my experience working with tens of thousands of entrepreneurs and business owners around the world, this is what usually happens. The people who go from being employee to being self-employed, the ones that make the jump, quit their job and give up the steady paycheck, often find themselves neck deep in stuff they didn't realize they were going to end up neck deep in when they started their own business. It can be a really scary step to take. It's a big jump. A lot changes.

These people begin with the intention to run their business different than their previous bosses ran the business they used to work for. But, when rubber meets the road, they don't really know what they're doing.

You can't do something very well if you don't know what you're doing. This is common sense. If I asked you to speak Portuguese right now, and you've never spoken Portuguese before in your life, you couldn't do it. Same idea with business.

Let's say you start your business, and you get your first client. Then you get your second client, and so on and so forth. As the ball gets rolling, you start to do business the way you know how to do business. This makes sense. Everyone does what they know.

But who taught you how to do business? Where did you learn how to do business from? You learned how to do business from watching your old bosses do it poorly. To put it bluntly, you learned how to do business from schmucks. So, now, you guessed it, you also start doing business like a schmuck. It's not your fault. It's just what you know.

Unless you train yourself. Unless you study by taking courses, reading books, getting support and hiring someone to guide you and coach you. If you don't do these things, you will just do what you know---and what you know is just how to do business like a schmuck.

Now, making the jump from employee to self-employed is a scary step, but it's not the hardest. I believe the hardest step is to go from self-employed to business owner. Business owner means you have a team of people working for you, hopefully a championship team of people. People you pay to perform, employees. But another option is you might work with a few self-employed people who you contract to do some of your work.

Here's a word of advice: speaking from my experience, self-employed people often feel entitled. They feel they are owed something. My experiences working with self-employed people haven't always been the best.

Really, what's best is if you can hire an in-house, championship team to support and continue growth. I highly recommend doing this if you have the resources and funds. Of course, there are going to be exceptions. Perhaps your business just doesn't require this. Keep in mind, with everything, a smart man understands a principle, but a wise man knows for every principle there is an exception. Common sense must always prevail.

A lot of people have trouble with this step, moving from self-employed to business owner, because they struggle with giving up control. They think, "Oh, nobody can do this stuff better than me." This is because for every move you make in business, there are going to be risks, and there are going to be rewards.

Yes, you might hire the wrong people sometimes. You are likely to kiss a few frogs on your path to success. Yes, you might be able to do a particular job better than a person you hire. But it's so important to invest in your team and allow them to grow and do their jobs. In the end, this is going to make your business much more sustainable. In the end, you may be able to simplify your tasks quite a lot. I'll explain.

I think there's a distinction Kiyosaki missed in his book. You see, my definition of a business owner is someone who works about an hour or two a week. They look at the reports, the income statements, and they have a meeting with the CEO, the managing director and the leadership team. That's what a business owner does.

But there's another category I call the business operator. The business operator is someone who is working day to day in the business. They are in the thick of it, just like everybody else.

If you're an entrepreneur that is passionate about your business, and you love it so much it makes you light up like a Christmas tree, then you should continue in the role of business operator. But make a distinction. You're not a business owner then. You're more in the business operator category.

Most business owners are actually business operators. I always ask my coaching clients, "Will your business pass the revolver test?" They normally ask for clarification on this.

So, I ask them, "If I were to put a revolver against your head and pull the trigger, and you were no more, what would happen to your business? Would it thrive or take a nosedive?"

Most of them admit it would take a nosedive! They are, therefore, business operators and not business owners. Remember, a business is simply a money-making machine that should be designed to operate and generate profits without you.

Next, let's talk about the investor. An investor is a person who puts up the cash, sits back and watches the game being played. For the average person, it's going to take a lot of time and effort before they can accumulate enough cash to play solely in this sector of the game. Most likely, you will become an investor as you are able to put up cash, and alongside that you will still do whatever else you do to generate your basic income.

The reason I'm telling you about all this stuff is because you've got to make a decision. You've got to decide how you want to play the game. Maybe you don't want to build a team. You don't want the headache. That's fine. But you've got to be conscious of where you're at, and you need to know what your approach is to playing the game.

As a self-employed person, are you really playing? Are you pretending to play? Are you playing not to lose? Are you playing on defense all the time? Are you winning at all? Are you winning on your own terms and conditions?

These are all very important questions to ask, but the key is, if you want to build true wealth, you've got be in business. If you want to create a life on your own terms, if you want to rebel against the status-quo and make something happen for yourself, business and entrepreneurship are the way to do it.

You've got to start playing the game of business.

# *Rebel Actions to Take*

- Identify how you want to play the game. Do you want to be an employee? Self-employed? Business operator? Business owner? Investor?
- Identify which one you are right now. Formulate a plan for how you will get to the point of being the one you want to be.
- How are you playing the game of business right now? Be honest with yourself. Make any adjustments necessary, and take action!

## *Rebel Words of Wisdom*

*"Business is simple and fun. Find out what they want, go get it, and then give it to them."*

Arnon Barnes

# Chapter 13

# Money Mastery and Education

---

Here is something really important you need to understand: wealthy people aren't smarter than you. They aren't necessarily better than you in any way. But one of the most important differences between the super successful and everybody else is they are excellent at money management. They know how to use their money. They know how to make their money work for them.

Awhile back, I had a client I was working with who I had been coaching for many years, and he was at the point where I had helped him make a tremendous amount of money. He was doing good business, serving people, adding value, having fun, and fulfilling his mission, but he was always late when paying my invoices.

This went on for a while, but it wasn't really at the forefront of my mind. I'm not the one who handles billing and all of that for my coaching business. I have an awesome team that handles this side of things for me.

Well, what happened was my team came to me, and they said, "Look, I know you've been working with this guy for years, but he is late on his payment every month. Every single month. He's even an entire month late sometimes. He's creating a lot of extra work for us, because we have to send him reminders and be on him all the time. Can you talk to him?"

Now, when my team came to me with that kind of request, of course, I wanted to talk to the guy. So, I went to him, and I said, "Look, what's going on? You know I don't talk to you about the money. I'm here to serve you and give you insights that change the game for you. So, what's really going on here? Why the late payments?"

I knew he'd been making stupid amounts of money. It's not like he wasn't able to pay the invoices and he always had to be stalling. Something else had to be going on.

As I started to ask him questions, he answered them, and I realized that even though he was making great money, he didn't have the concept of money mastery down. He had no clue how to manage his money.

People always say, "It's not how much you make. It's how much you keep." Right? Well, I want to turn that on its head; it's not how much you keep. It's what you do with what you keep.

Years ago there was a UPS driver named Theodore Johnson who never earned more than $14,000 a year. From that, he paid his mortgage, bought food, paid for his car and the like. You wouldn't expect a person making this kind of money to end up very wealthy. But by the time he died, he had amassed a whopping $70 million! How did he do it? Money mastery.

Money mastery is the art of telling your money what to do and not the other way around. It means if you earn one dollar, you take 20, 30 or even 50 cents of that, and you set it aside to put into an investment. But investing is not the only part of money mastery that's important. Most people know to be setting money aside for later in life, even if they don't do it.

But a lot of people don't know how to enjoy their money. Yeah, they might make a lot of money, but they always feel guilty about spending it. This is why it's really important to put money into a fun account or a holiday account, money you can spend to enjoy life, guilt-free.

Let's say you make $5,000 providing services or products or whatever to a client. Now, you've got your bills to pay and your investments to make, but if you put 5 percent of what you made into this holiday account, eventually that's going to add up. You're going to look at that account one day and say, "Wow, I've got six grand in here! I'm going to go on a cruise around the world for a month."

You really can do this type of stuff guilt-free. Because what you're spending is money you've purposed to spend. This is real money mastery. You want to enjoy life. You deserve to enjoy life. Let me tell you, just watching the numbers rack up in your bank account might give you an adrenaline rush at first, but if you don't set some of that money aside to nurture your inner child, shit's going to hit the fan for you pretty fast.

You're going to end up working too much, and at some point you're probably going to hit a wall. You need balance. You need to have fun with your money the responsible, guilt-free way.

Money mastery is one of the most powerful, yet forgotten skills of entrepreneurs. It doesn't matter how much you make or how much you keep, the secret is what you do with it. This way of thinking is a game changer in and of itself. This key can change everything for you, your family, your business and your life.

I know what you're thinking. Life is not all about fun and games. And that's true. That's why all high achievers understand they must also set aside money to invest in their education.

Every single wealthy person invests in their education. They're always reading another book. They're always taking another course. They're always attending another seminar. They're always buying online programs. They all invest in business or success coaching.

Whether it's learning another language, learning about business, learning about accounting, or learning how to communicate with power and clarity, high achievers are always learning something. They are students for life. They realize education is a must.

Here's why. Think of yourself as a container. If you're a small container, how much money can you hold? Not much. But when you educate yourself, you grow. You, as a container, grow. A big container can simply hold bigger money. A little container will hold little money. This is very, very simple, and most people know it to be true. But the thing is, most people don't act on this knowledge.

They get too busy. They're too busy doing things that don't work instead of taking the time to educate themselves about what does work. That's why you reading this book is such an amazing thing for you to be doing. If you've gotten to this point in this book, you've invested in yourself. You've taken the time to enlarge your container so it can hold more and more.

Whether you knew it or not when you picked this book up, you have already taken a very important step towards success as a *Rebel Entrepreneur.*

# *Rebel Actions to Take*

- Do you have money mastery down? Remember, it's not what you keep. It's what you do with what you keep.
- Do you have a holiday account? Are you enriching your life with what you earn, or are you just racking up numbers in a bank account?
- Take time to get your priorities straight. Investing in education is always a good idea! Remember, a big container can hold big money! A small container only holds small money.

## *Rebel Words of Wisdom*

*"The man that doesn't read the books, has no advantage over the man that doesn't even know how to read them. Readers are leaders."*

Arnon Barnes

# Chapter 14

# Get a Coach!

---

This is the very last key to success I'm going to talk about. And, yes, I saved the best for last. This is something every successful person on planet earth knows and follows. I promise you. It doesn't matter if we're talking about a tennis champion, a soccer champion, a running champion, a swimming champion, or a champion of industry, one of the things you must absolutely have to be successful is a coach.

By this, I mean a coach you're paying for. Not somebody who is just going to help you out for free every once in awhile when they have an extra minute to spare. Not someone who is just going to let you off the hook when you don't bother to do your homework, or when you barely show up, or when you show up with all kinds of excuses.

Here's the truth: the more expensive your coach is, the better. Because the more money you put on the table, the more committed you're going to be. If you put down $500 for a coach, you will play at the $500 level.

To be quite honest and vulnerable, I pay thousands and thousands of dollars for my coaches. Because I know when I pay that kind of money, my commitment level is going to be sky high. And when my commitment level is sky high, I get sky high results.

Most people live with this concept of "good enough." They think, "I'm happy enough. I'm successful enough. I'm doing good enough." But I'm here to tell you today: good enough is overrated. Good enough is bullshit. Good enough is a waste of your precious energy, your time and your gift.

Good enough is playing small. Even worse, saying something is "good enough" is like justifying mediocrity. It's like saying you're alright with just playing the game and letting other people pass you up year after year. It's almost like giving up, like just getting by.

Listen, it is your duty to become successful. It is your responsibility to take care of you, your family, and your tribe, your community. So, my questions for you are these: who's pushing you? Who's making things uncomfortable for you? Who's challenging you? Who's pissing you off on a weekly basis? Who's stretching you? Who's asking you the tough questions? You know, the questions you don't want to hear but know will serve you.

When I hire a coach, I say to them, "Look, I'm not looking for a friend." When I coach my clients, I tell them, "I am not here to be your friend. I'm here to be your best friend, because your best friend always tells you the truth."

Because when you know the truth, you can work to get things going in the right direction. When you have the truth, you can go places. When you have the truth, you can adjust. You can change. You can amend. You can adapt. You can correct things. You can truly succeed in every way imaginable.

We all have blind spots. We all have things about us we can't see. Every single one of us, me included. A good, experienced coach can see these things in you, and make it so you can see them, too. Often it is the things we can't see that are the things holding us back.

When things aren't going right for us in life or in business, we often feel like we're fighting some invisible enemy, because we are! We can't see in all directions. We don't have eyes in the backs of our heads. We all need someone to point out what's really going on and to help us correct it.

So, why don't most people have a coach? Because most people (not you, of course) feel like asking for help is a weakness. That's why most entrepreneurs never succeed big.

In fact, over 80 percent of businesses crash and burn and go bankrupt within their first two years. Less than 0.4 percent of businesses ever make more than $5 million in a single financial year. Why does this happen? Why do businesses never fully take off? Why do they fail so regularly?

Because business owners don't know what they don't know. You don't know what you don't know. And what you don't know will cost you. It will cost you big time. It will cost you energy, and it will cost you money. Lots of it. I guarantee you that. If you think you're saving money by not getting a coach, you're in for a rude awakening down the line.

I've had clients tell me, straight up, that they wish they had gotten coached by me ten years earlier than they did. After working with me and going through my coaching programs, one specific client shared with me that she was working in her business 20 hours less every week. You'd think this would mean she wasn't making as much money as she was when she was working those 20 hours, right? Wrong.

In just one coaching session with me, we pinpointed an area in her business where she was leaving, every year, £109k of cash money on the table. Over the course of ten years, that amounts to well over 1 million pounds!

So, let me ask you, was her hiring me to coach her worth it? She definitely thinks so.

Remember, if you don't want to get coached, and you refuse to educate yourself, then the marketplace will educate you. The type of education the marketplace will give you, my friend, is way more expensive than the amount any coach is ever going to cost you. The marketplace is ruthless. It is no respecter of persons, and it certainly isn't your best friend unless you know how to relate to it. And that's very, very tough to do without help.

Here's the thing. You could spend years of your time, your life and millions of your hard-earned dollars trying to make your business work on your own. But the truth is, even then, things might not work out for you.

Throughout this book, we've talked a lot about what it takes to be successful, and we've already established that success is possible for you. But I've got to make a really important point here, so don't miss it.

Any one of the success principles we've talked about throughout this book cannot make things happen for you on its own. You need the full arsenal of weaponry at your disposal if you want to win this battle. Because I'll tell you right now, if you want to fight the system, if you want to break off the chains that keep you trapped in a dead-end job or in a failing business, you better have your armory fully stocked.

Look, we all have to go through some temporary pain. But at the end of that pain, there is always growth. Pain is inevitable, but suffering is a choice. Bottom line, get a coach. The more expensive the better.

There are plenty of people out there that are going to come up against you. Fake people who say they're going to help you out and end up doing you harm. People who don't believe you could ever make it and bad mouth you every step of the way. People who are lazy and whose laziness, if you choose to be around it, will rub off on you and almost guarantee you're not going to succeed.

This is why, if you want to be a *Rebel Entrepreneur*, you need a coach. You need somebody who will fight with you. Because if you're reading this book right now, I can guarantee you the life you've chosen, the life of an entrepreneur, is not the easiest one you could have chosen for yourself. In fact, being an entrepreneur is a lonely journey. That's why having a support system and having someone on your team you can confide in, someone who wants to see you win big, is imperative.

As someone who works with people, day in and day out, people who have chosen to take the same path you have, I can tell you from observing their success and enjoying my own in this very same sphere…

*It's worth it.*

# *Rebel Actions to Take*

- **This one is simple, but very important. Get a coach!**

JOIN THE

# BUSINESS REBEL MASTERCLASS™

- **FOCUS on what's most important**
- **Speed up your Business Growth**
- **Get Unstuck**
- **Build Your WINNING Mindset**
- **Create a Championship Team**
- **Increase your Confidence**
- **Make More Money!**

For Tickets, Go To

# www.BUSINESS**REBEL**MASTERCLASS.com

"In life and in business, you either win or you learn.  Let's win."

# Arnon Barnes
REBEL ENTREPRENEUR

JOIN MY SIGNATURE PROGRAM

## BUSINESS REBEL MASTERCLASS™ FOR ENTREPRENEURS

## THIS IS WHAT YOU WILL LEARN

- **FOCUS on what's most important**
- **Speed up your Business Growth**
- **Get Unstuck**
- **Build Your WINNING Mindset**
- **Create a Championship Team**
- **Increase your Confidence**
- **Make More Money!**

For more information, visit:

www.BUSINESS**REBEL**MASTERCLASS.com

AFFIRM

21.36
24.44
124.55
88.59
65.42
111.48

+ 400.00
+ 200.00

Made in the USA
Monee, IL
07 April 2025

15315304R00069